# MARVELOUS MAPS AND GRAPHS

## Practical Worksheets for Grades 1-3

Written and Illustrated
by
**Ginger Wentrcek**

**MAKEMASTER® Blackline Masters**

**Fearon Teacher Aids**
Carthage, Illinois

ISBN-0-8224-6332-6
Printed in the United States of America.

l.9 8 7 6 5 4 3 2 1

# **Which Direction?**

North

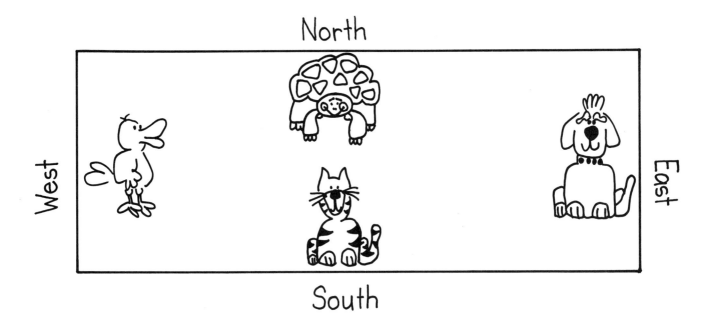

West

East

South

Look at the map above. Underline each sentence below that is true.

1. The cat is south of the turtle.

2. The turtle is east of the dog.

3. The bird is north of the turtle.

4. The dog is east of the bird.

5. The turtle is north of the cat.

6. The bird is west of the dog.

7. The cat is north of the dog.

8. The dog is south of the cat.

# Finding Your Way

Fill in the blanks below.  Use these words: north, south, east, or west.

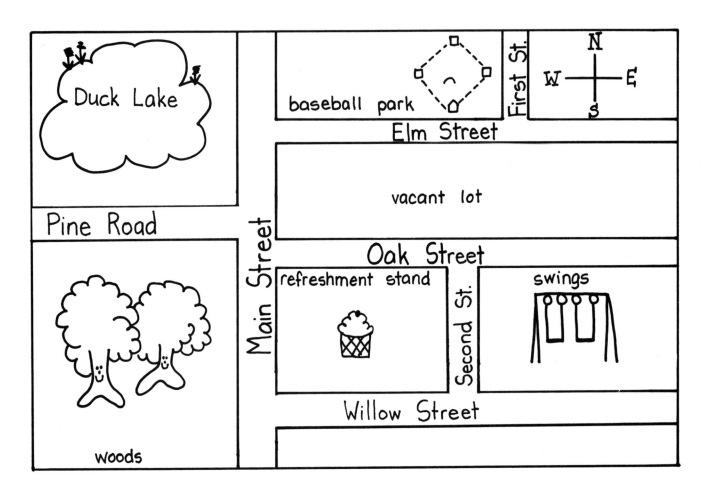

1. The baseball park is _____ of the vacant lot.

2. The swings are _____ of the refreshment stand.

3. The woods are _____ of Duck Lake.

4. Duck Lake is _____ of Elm Street.

# Islands in the Sea

North

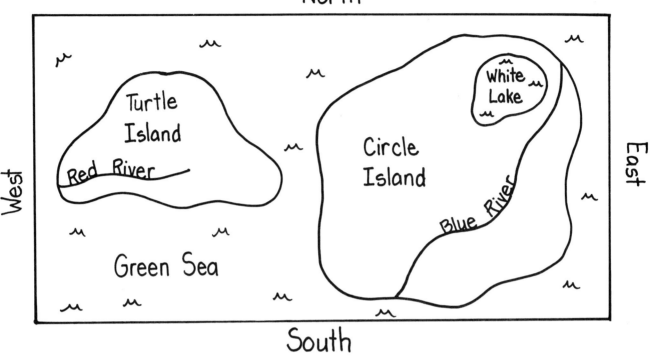

South

Look at the map and fill in the blanks below.

1. _____ Island is bigger than _____ Island.

2. Turtle Island is _____ of Circle Island.

3. The _____ Sea surrounds both islands.

4. White Lake is on _____ Island.

5. The _____ River is longer than the _____ River.

6. Circle Island is _____ of Turtle Island.

# Pirate's Map

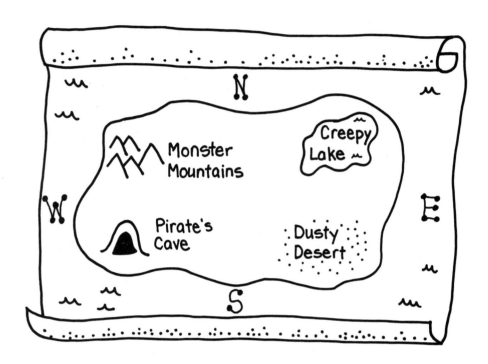

Fill in the blanks below to tell map directions.

1. Creepy Lake is _____ of Pirate's Cave.

2. Dusty Desert is _____ of Pirate's Cave.

3. Monster Mountains are _____ of Dusty Desert.

4. Pirate's Cave is _____ of Creepy Lake.

5. Creepy Lake is _____ of Dusty Desert.

6. Monster Mountains are _____ of Creepy Lake.

7. Dusty Desert is _____ of Monster Mountains.

8. Pirate's Cave is _____ of Monster Mountains.

Marvelous Maps and Graphs, copyright © 1984

# Using Symbols

Use the map to complete the work below.

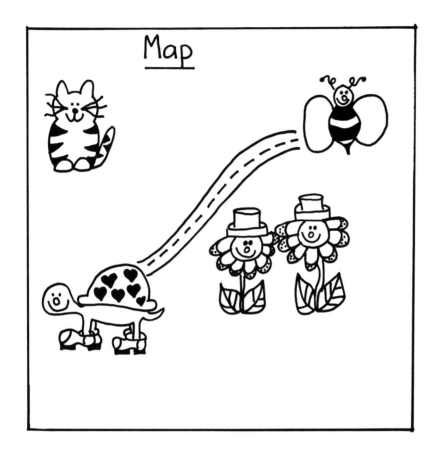 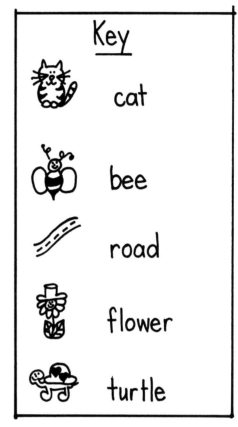

1. There are two _____ by the road.

2. A _____ is across the road from the flowers.

3. The road goes from the turtle to a _____ .

4. Are there any dogs near the road? _____

5. Color the road green.

6. With a red crayon, draw one line under the bee.

# Symbol Sense

Look at the map and complete the work below.

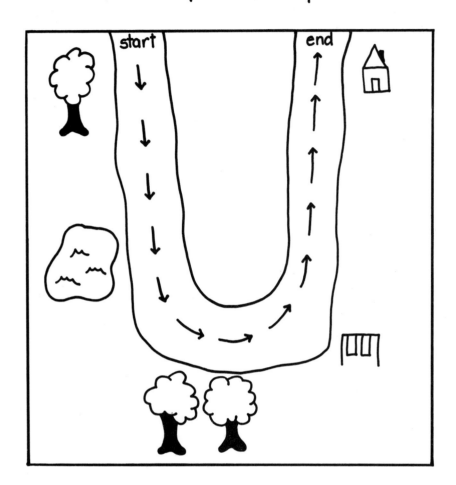

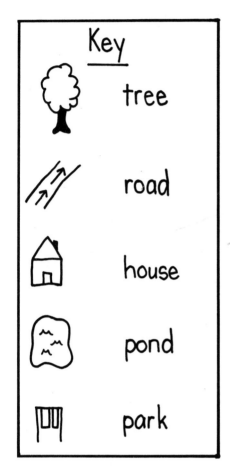

1. There are _____ trees.

2. A _____ is at the end of the road.

3. A _____ is after the first tree.

4. A _____ is after the park.

5. Draw a pond between the park and the house.

6. Color the road blue.

Name _____

# Going Through the City

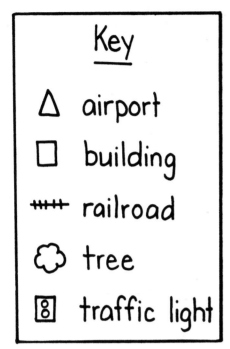

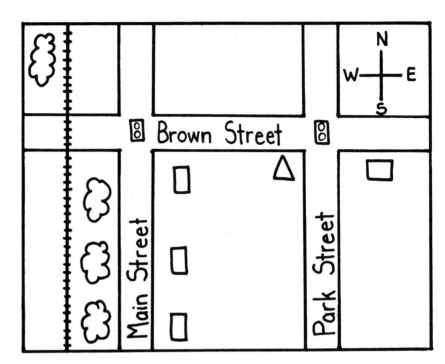

Look at the map and answer these questions.

1. How many buildings are there? _____

2. What two streets does the airport touch?

   _____   _____

3. What street does the railroad cross? _____

4. How many trees are east of the railroad? _____

5. On what street are both traffic lights located?

   _____

6. What streets are shown on the map? _____

   _____   _____

# Beginning Sectors

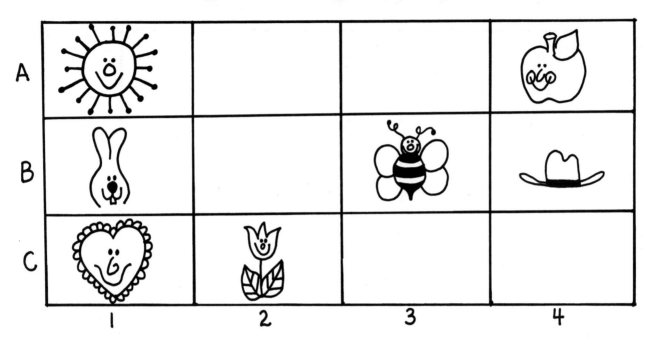

Complete the work below.

1. The _____ is in A1.

2. A _____ is in B3.

3. A cowboy hat is in _____.

4. An apple is in _____.

5. A rabbit is in _____.

6. A _____ is in C2.

7. Make a red "X" in A3.

8. Make a blue "O" in C4.

*Marvelous Maps and Graphs,* copyright © 1984

# Sector Sillies

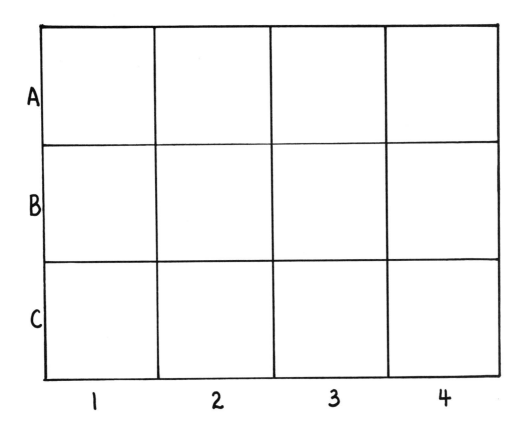

Cut and paste each square below in the sector indicated above each person.

C3

B1

A4

B2

A1

C4

A3

B4

# Sector Sense

### Key

 mountain

lake

capital city

• city

desert

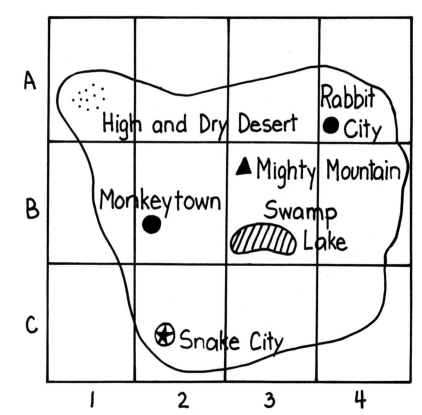

Look at the map and complete the sentences below.

1. The capital city is _____. It is in sector _____.

2. High and Dry is a _____.

3. Swamp Lake is in sector _____.

4. Mighty is a _____. It is in sector _____.

5. There are _____ cities on the map.

6. _____ is in sector B2.

# Reviewing Sectors and Symbols

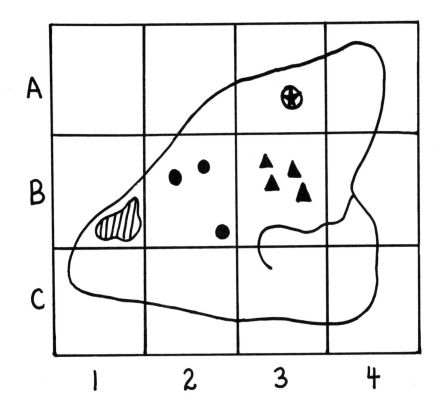

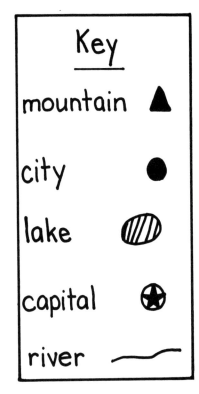

Key

mountain ▲

city ●

lake ◓

capital ✪

river 〜

Look at the map and complete each sentence.

1. The mountains are in sector _____.

2. The river begins in sector C3 and ends in sector _____.

3. Three _____ are in sector B2.

4. A lake is in sector _____.

5. The river goes through sectors _____, _____, and _____.

6. The capital city is in sector _____.

# How Long?

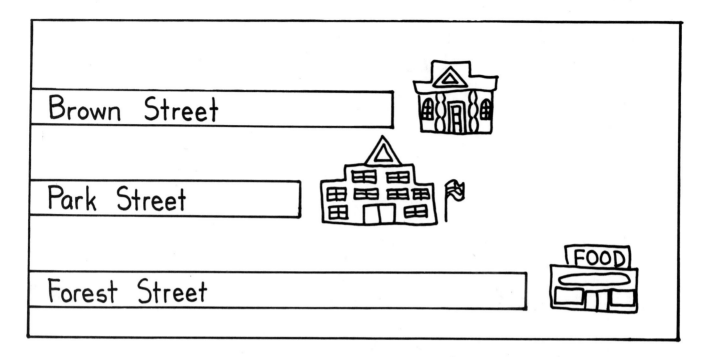

Scale in miles :

```
0       2       4       6       8
L___|___|___|___|___|___|___|___
```

Use the scale and complete each sentence below.

1. Brown Street is _____ miles long.

2. _____ is the shortest street.

3. Forest Street is _____ miles long.

4. _____ is six miles long.

5. Forest Street and Park Street are _____ miles long altogether.

6. _____ is the longest street.

# Let's Go Fishing

Use the scale. Tell how far it is from:

1. Jellyfish to octopus _____

2. Starfish to fish _____

3. Fish to jellyfish _____

4. Octopus to fish _____

5. Jellyfish to fish to octopus _____

6. Octopus to fish to starfish _____

Scale: 1 inch = 10 feet

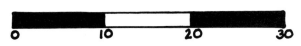

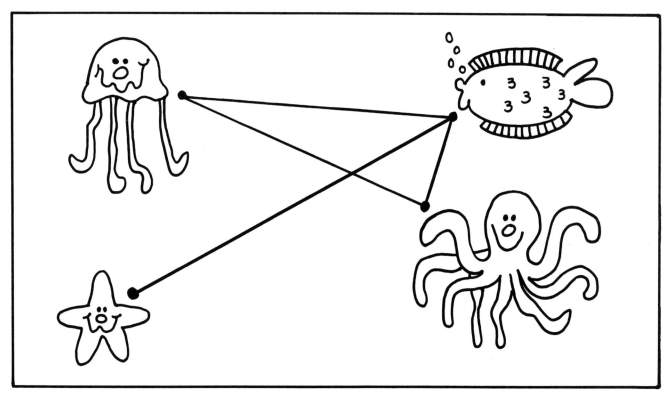

Name _____

# How Many Miles?

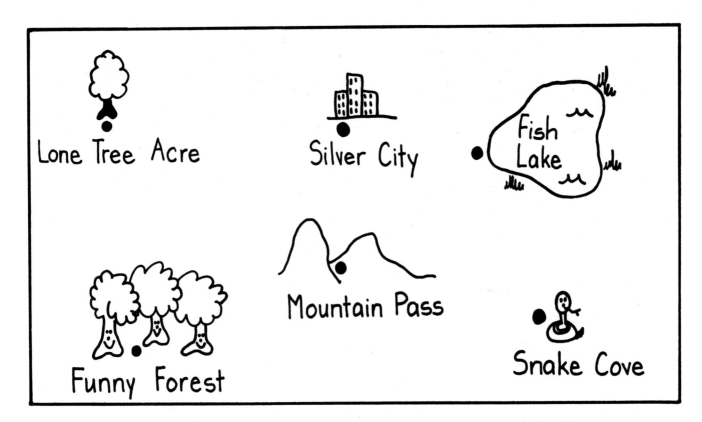

Scale in miles: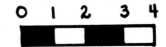

Use the scale. Measure between the dots on the map above. Tell how many miles it is from:

1. Lone Tree Acre to Mountain Pass _____

2. Mountain Pass to Silver City _____

3. Fish Lake to Snake Cove _____

4. Funny Forest to Silver City _____

5. Snake Cove to Funny Forest _____

14

Marvelous Maps and Graphs, copyright © 1984

# Circus Delights

Scale in yards

0  1  2  3  4

Measure between the dots and use the scale to complete these sentences.

1. The circus tent is in sector _____.

2. A _____ is in sector A1.

3. Three balloons are in sector _____.

4. It is _____ yards from the seal to the lion's cage.

5. It is _____ yards from the seal to the clown.

6. It is _____ yards from the clown to the monkey.

7. Draw an elephant in sector B4.

# Barnyard Fun

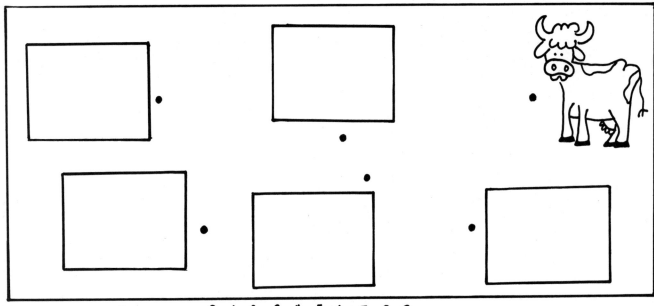

Scale in feet: 0 1 2 3 4 5 6 7 8 9

Use the scale and measure between the dots. Cut out the animals below. Glue the:

1. horse 17 feet from the cow

2. rooster 10 feet from the horse

3. barn 8 feet from the rooster

4. dog 12 feet from the barn

5. sheep 7 feet from the dog

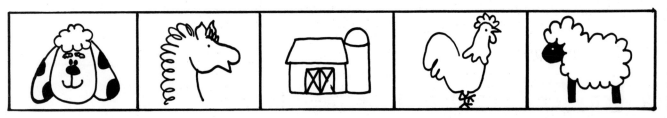

# Reading a Map

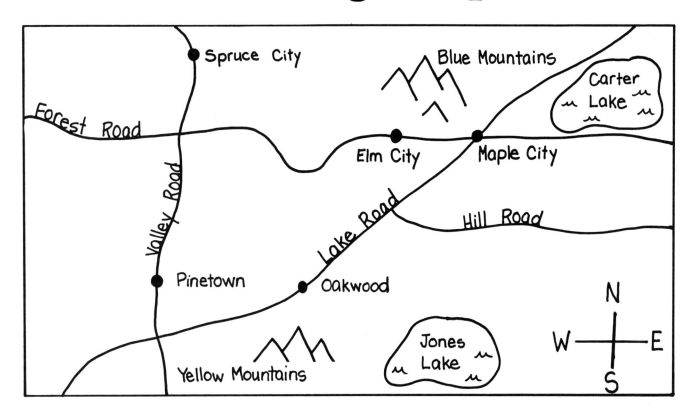

Use the map to complete the sentences.

1. _____ Road runs north and south.

2. _____ Lake is between Lake Road and Forest Road.

3. _____ City is at the place where Lake Road and Forest Road cross.

4. The _____ Mountains are south of Oakwood.

5. There are no towns on _____ Road.

6. _____ City is closest to Maple City.

Marvelous Maps and Graphs, copyright © 1984

# How Old Are You?

| Name | Age |
|------|-----|
| Wendy | 9 |
| Susan | 6 |
| Wanda | 8 |
| Jan | 7 |
| Barry | 4 |
| Dan | 5 |

Use the table to complete the sentences.

1. _____ is 7 years old.

2. _____ is 5 years old.

3. Susan is _____ years old.

4. Wanda is _____ years old.

5. _____ is the youngest child.

6. _____ is the oldest child.

7. Jan and Susan are _____ years old altogether.

Name _____

# Pet Parade

Look at the chart. Then fill in the blanks below.

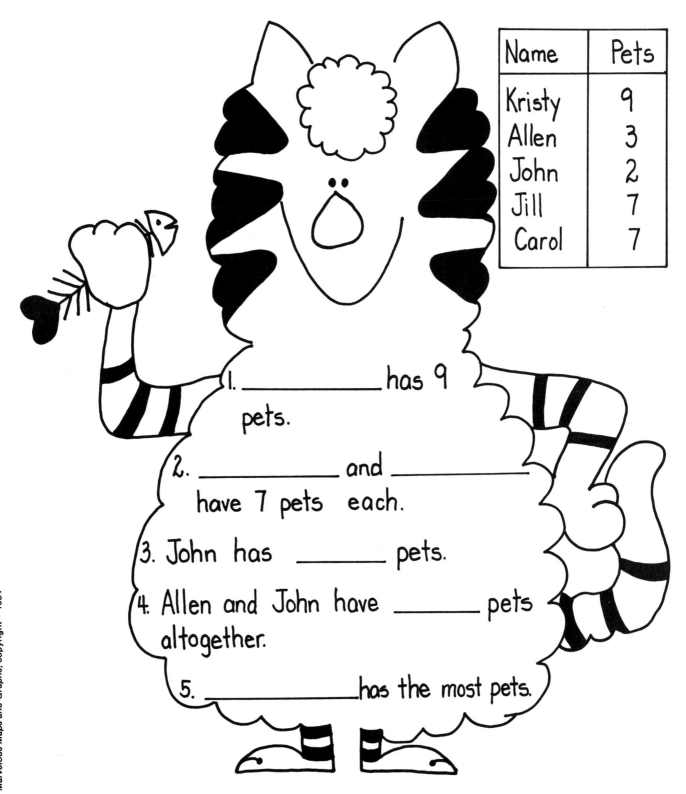

| Name | Pets |
|------|------|
| Kristy | 9 |
| Allen | 3 |
| John | 2 |
| Jill | 7 |
| Carol | 7 |

1. _____ has 9 pets.

2. _____ and _____ have 7 pets each.

3. John has _____ pets.

4. Allen and John have _____ pets altogether.

5. _____ has the most pets.

Name _____

# Flying High

Read the table and complete the work below.

| Name | Toy | Number |
|------|-----|--------|
| Mary | doll | 5 |
| Ernie | kite | 2 |
| Ginger | blocks | 9 |
| Nancy | ball | 4 |

1. Mary has _____ dolls.

2. Ginger has nine _____.

3. _____ has two kites.

4. Nancy has _____ balls.

5. _____ has the most toys.

6. Mary and Ernie have _____ toys altogether.

7. Ginger has _____ more toys than Nancy has.

Name_____

# Our Pets

The table shows the types of pets the children own. Study the table and complete the sentences below.

|  | Birds | Cats | Dogs |
|---|---|---|---|
| Tim | 7 | 0 | 0 |
| Sue | 2 | 5 | 3 |
| Lee | 1 | 1 | 2 |

1. Tim has _____ birds.

2. Lee has _____ cat.

3. Sue has _____ dogs.

4. _____ has more cats than Lee has.

5. _____ has the most birds.

6. Sue has _____ pets altogether.

7. _____ has the most pets altogether.

8. _____ has the most cats.

9. _____ has the fewest birds.

10. _____ has fewer dogs than Lee has.

Name _____

# Going to the Circus

The table below tells what time the circus starts and ends. Study the table and answer the questions below.

| Day | Start | End |
|---|---|---|
| Sunday | 6:00 | 8:00 |
| Mon.-Wed. | Closed | |
| Thursday | 5:30 | 7:00 |
| Friday | 6:30 | 8:30 |
| Saturday | 7:00 | 9:30 |

1. If you missed the show Sunday, what day could you attend the next show? _____

2. On what day does the show last the longest amount of time? _____

3. How many weekdays does the circus perform?
_____

4. How many hours does the circus last on Sunday?
_____

5. If you had to be in bed by 8 P.M., could you go to the circus Friday? _____ Why or why not?

_____

# Basketball Shootout

The graph shows how many points four members of the Bombers basketball team scored. Read the graph and complete each sentence below.

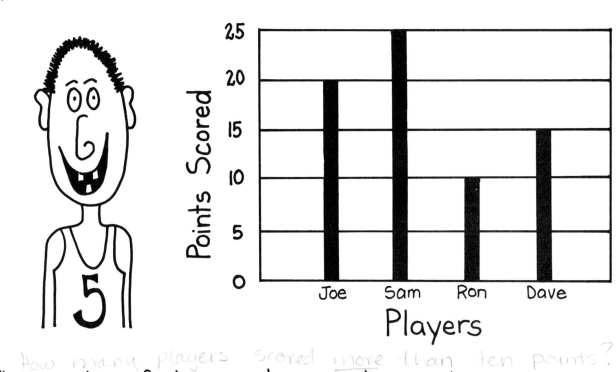

Points Scored

Joe  Sam  Ron  Dave

Players

1. *How many players scored more than ten points?*
   The number of players who scored more than 10 points is _____.

2. *Who scored the most points?*
   _____ scored the most points.

3. *How many points did Dave score.*
   Dave scored _____ points.

4. _____ and _____ scored less than 16 points.

5. *Joe and Sam scored how many points all together?*
   Sam and Ron scored _____ points altogether.

6. *Who scored 15 points?*
   _____ scored 15 points.

23

# Ride 'Em Cowboy

Study the graph. Answer the questions below.

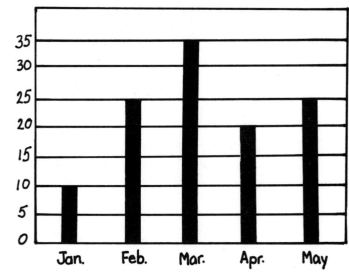

Number of Cowboys Working at the W̄ Ranch

Months

1. During what month did the fewest number of cowboys work at the W̄ Ranch? _____

2. During which two months did the same number of cowboys work at the W̄ Ranch? _____

3. During which month did 20 cowboys work at the W̄ Ranch? _____

4. During which month did the greatest number of cowboys work at the W̄ Ranch? _____

5. How many cowboys worked during February and May?

_____

Name_____

# Bessie Takes a Walk

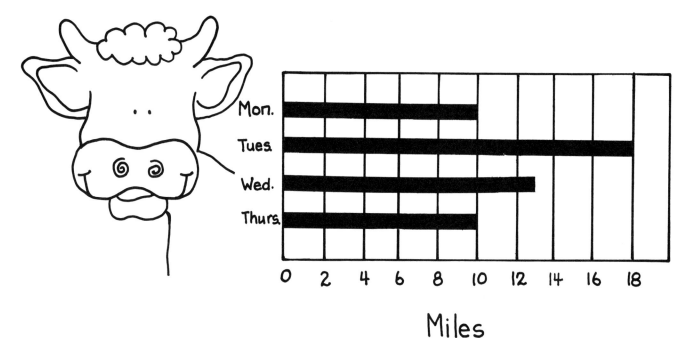

Miles

The graph tells how many miles Bessie walked.
Read the graph and complete the sentences below.

How many miles did Bessie walk on Thurs.?

1. Bessie walked _____ miles Thursday.

" " " " " " " " " Wed.?

2. Bessie walked _____ miles Wednesday.

On what day did Bessie walk the farthest?

3. She walked the farthest on _____.

What days did Bessie walk the amount?

4. She walked the same distance on _____
and _____.

How many miles did Bessie walk altogether on Mon.& Wed.?

5. Bessie walked _____ miles on Monday and
Wednesday altogether.

6. The graph shows how far Bessie walked on Tuesday,
_____, _____, and _____.

# What's Cooking?

Study the line graph. Then answer the questions that follow.

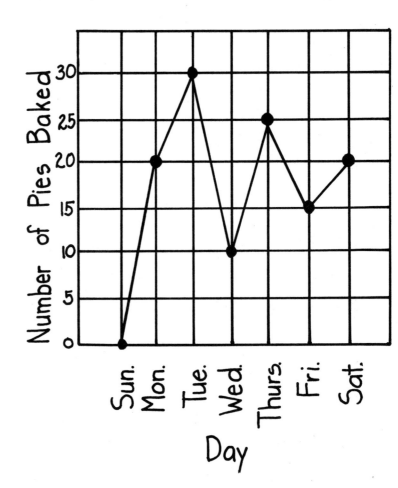

1. How many pies did Cooky bake Wednesday? _____

2. When were the most pies baked? _____

3. On which days were the same number of pies baked?
   _____     _____

4. Altogether, how many pies were baked on Thursday and Saturday? _____

# Under the Big Top

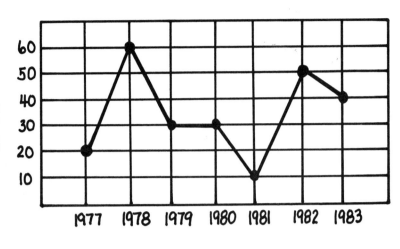

Year

Study the graph above. Answer the following questions.

1. How many clowns worked at the circus in 1982 ? _____

2. In which year did the fewest clowns work at the Big Top Circus ? _____

3. For how many years does the graph tell about clowns working at the circus ? _____

4. During which years did the same number of clowns work at the circus ? _____  _____

5. How many clowns worked at the circus in 1982 and 1983 altogether ? _____

6. In which year did 50 clowns work at the Big Top Circus ? _____

# Kids' Colors

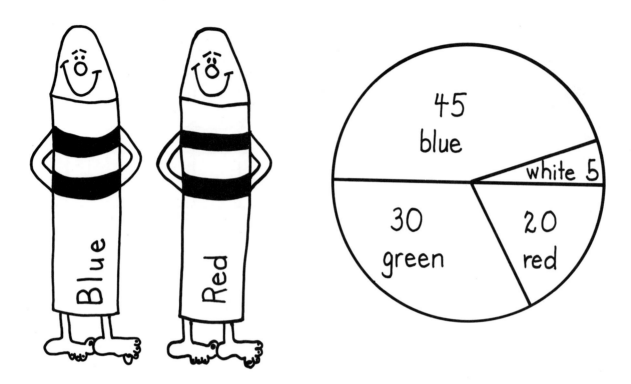

Study the circle graph. Each part tells about one color children like. Use the circle graph to fill in the blanks below.

1. The greatest number of children like _____.

2. There are 20 children who like _____.

3. The least number of children like _____.

4. _____ more children like blue than like green.

5. _____ children like green.

6. There are more children who like _____ than there are who like green.

Marvelous Maps and Graphs, copyright © 1984

# Our Favorite Animals

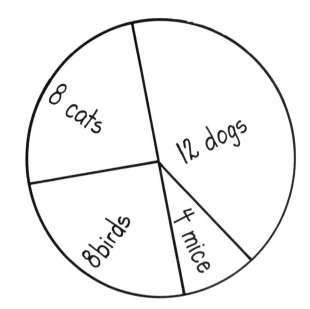

8 cats

12 dogs

8 birds

4 mice

The circle graph shows each of Mrs. Smith's students' favorite animal. Look at the graph and complete each sentence.

1. The most popular animal is the _____.

2. Only _____ children like mice.

3. The same number of children like cats as like _____.

4. More children like _____ than like birds.

5. Fewer children like _____ than like cats.

6. There are _____ more children who like dogs better than cats.

7. There are _____ children in Mrs. Smith's room.

# Answer Key

**Which Direction?,** p. 1

    1. ;   4. ;   5. ;   6.

**Finding Your Way,** p. 2

    1. north;   2. east;   3. south;   4. west

**Islands in the Sea,** p. 3

    1. Circle/Turtle;   2. west;   3. Green;

    4. Circle;   5. Blue/Red;   6. east

**Pirate's Map,** p. 4

    1. northeast;   2. east;   3. northwest;

    4. southwest;   5. north;   6. west;

    7. southeast;   8. south

**Using Symbols,** p. 5

    1. flowers;   2. cat;   3. bee;   4. no

**Symbol Sense,** p. 6

    1. 3;   2. house;   3. pond;   4. house

**Going Through the City,** p. 7

    1. 4;   2. Brown Street/Park Street;   3. Brown Street;   4. 3;   5. Brown Street;   6. Brown Street/Main Street/Park Street

**Beginning Sectors,** p. 8

    1. sun;   2. bee;   3. B4;   4. A4;   5. B1;

    6. tulip

**Sector Sillies,** p. 9

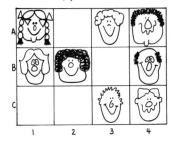

**Sector Sense,** p. 10

    1. Snake City/C2;   2. dessert;   3. B3;

    4. mountain/B3;   5. 3;   6. Monkeytown

**Reviewing Sectors and Symbols,** p. 11

    1. B3;   2. B4;   3. cities;   4. B1;

    5. C3, B3, B4;   6. A3

**How Long?,** p. 12

    1. 8;   2. Park Street;   3. 11;   4. Park Street;

    5. 17;   6. Forest Street

**Let's Go Fishing,** p. 13

    1. 30 feet;   2. 40 feet;   3. 30 feet;   4. 10 feet;

    5. 40 feet;   6. 50 feet

**How Many Miles?,** p. 14

    1. 8 miles;   2. 4 miles;   3. 5 miles;   4. 9 miles;

    5. 12 miles

**Circus Delights,** p. 15

    1. C1;   2. clown;   3. B2;   4. 7;   5. 9;   6. 5

**Barnyard Fun,** p. 16

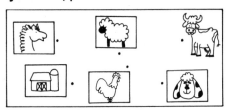

**Reading a Map,** p. 17

    1. Valley;   2. Carter;   3. Maple;   4. Yellow;

    5. Hill;   6. Elm

**How Old Are You?,** p. 18

    1. Jan;   2. Dan;   3. 6;   4. 8;   5. Barry;

    6. Wendy;   7. 13

**Pet Parade,** p. 19

    1. Kristy;   2. Jill/Carol;   3. 2;   4. 5;   5. Kristy

**Flying High,** p. 20

    1. 5;   2. blocks;   3. Ernie;   4. 4;   5. Ginger;

    6. 7;   7. 5

**Our Pets,** p. 21

    1. 7;   2. 1;   3. 3;   4. Sue;   5. Tim;   6. 10;

    7. Sue;   8. Sue;   9. Lee;   10. Tim

**Going to the Circus,** p. 22

    1. Thursday;   2. Saturday;   3. 2;   4. 2;

    5. No. The show lasts until 8:30. (Or: Yes. But I would have to leave early.)

**Basketball Shootout,** p. 23

    1. 3;   2. Sam;   3. 15;   4. Ron/Dave;   5. 35;

    6. Dave

**Ride 'Em Cowboy,** p. 24

    1. Jan.;   2. Feb. and May;   3. Apr.;   4. Mar.;

    5. 25

**Bessie Takes a Walk,** p. 25

    1. 10;   2. 13;   3. Tues.;   4. Mon./Thurs.;

    5. 23;   6. Mon., Wed., Thurs.

**What's Cooking?,** p.26

    1. 10;   2. Tue.;   3. Mon./Sat.;   4. 45

**Under the Big Top,** p. 27

    1. 50;   2. 1981;   3. 7;   4. 1979/1980;   5. 90;

    6. 1982

**Kids' Colors,** p. 28

    1. blue;   2. red;   3. white;   4. 15;   5. 30;

    6. blue

**Our Favorite Animals,** p. 29

    1. dog;   2. 4;   3. birds;   4. dogs;   5. mice;

    6. 4;   7. 32